Fixed Assets Depreciation Log

Fixed Assets Depreciation

Period: ______________________________

Asset Description	Date of Acquisition	Original Price	Current Value	Depreciatio n Amount	Current Book Value

Fixed Assets Depreciation

Period: ______________________________

Asset Description	Date of Acquisition	Original Price	Current Value	Depreciatio n Amount	Current Book Value

Fixed Assets Depreciation

Period: ______________________________

Asset Description	Date of Acquisition	Original Price	Current Value	Depreciation Amount	Current Book Value

Fixed Assets Depreciation

Period: ______________________________

Asset Description	Date of Acquisition	Original Price	Current Value	Depreciation Amount	Current Book Value

Fixed Assets Depreciation

Period: ____________________________

Asset Description	Date of Acquisition	Original Price	Current Value	Depreciation Amount	Current Book Value

Fixed Assets Depreciation

Period: ______________________________

Asset Description	Date of Acquisition	Original Price	Current Value	Depreciation Amount	Current Book Value

Fixed Assets Depreciation

Period: ______________________________

Asset Description	Date of Acquisition	Original Price	Current Value	Depreciatio n Amount	Current Book Value

Fixed Assets Depreciation

Period: ______________________________

Asset Description	Date of Acquisition	Original Price	Current Value	Depreciatio n Amount	Current Book Value

Fixed Assets Depreciation

Period: ____________________________

Asset Description	Date of Acquisition	Original Price	Current Value	Depreciation Amount	Current Book Value

Fixed Assets Depreciation

Period: ______________________________

Asset Description	Date of Acquisition	Original Price	Current Value	Depreciation Amount	Current Book Value

Fixed Assets Depreciation

Period: ____________________________

Asset Description	Date of Acquisition	Original Price	Current Value	Depreciatio n Amount	Current Book Value

Fixed Assets Depreciation

Period: ______________________________

Asset Description	Date of Acquisition	Original Price	Current Value	Depreciatio n Amount	Current Book Value

Fixed Assets Depreciation

Period: ______________________________

Asset Description	Date of Acquisition	Original Price	Current Value	Depreciation Amount	Current Book Value

Fixed Assets Depreciation

Period: ______________________________

Asset Description	Date of Acquisition	Original Price	Current Value	Depreciation Amount	Current Book Value

Fixed Assets Depreciation

Period: ______________________________

Asset Description	Date of Acquisition	Original Price	Current Value	Depreciation Amount	Current Book Value

Fixed Assets Depreciation

Period: ______________________________

Asset Description	Date of Acquisition	Original Price	Current Value	Depreciation Amount	Current Book Value

Fixed Assets Depreciation

Period: ____________________________

Asset Description	Date of Acquisition	Original Price	Current Value	Depreciatio n Amount	Current Book Value

Fixed Assets Depreciation

Period: ____________________________

Asset Description	Date of Acquisition	Original Price	Current Value	Depreciation Amount	Current Book Value

Fixed Assets Depreciation

Period: ______________________________

Asset Description	Date of Acquisition	Original Price	Current Value	Depreciation Amount	Current Book Value

Fixed Assets Depreciation

Period: ______________________________

Asset Description	Date of Acquisition	Original Price	Current Value	Depreciatio n Amount	Current Book Value

Fixed Assets Depreciation

Period: ______________________________

Asset Description	Date of Acquisition	Original Price	Current Value	Depreciation Amount	Current Book Value

Fixed Assets Depreciation

Period: ______________________________

Asset Description	Date of Acquisition	Original Price	Current Value	Depreciation Amount	Current Book Value

Fixed Assets Depreciation

Period: ____________________________

Asset Description	Date of Acquisition	Original Price	Current Value	Depreciatio n Amount	Current Book Value

Fixed Assets Depreciation

Period: ______________________________

Asset Description	Date of Acquisition	Original Price	Current Value	Depreciation Amount	Current Book Value

Fixed Assets Depreciation

Period: ______________________________

Asset Description	Date of Acquisition	Original Price	Current Value	Depreciation Amount	Current Book Value

Fixed Assets Depreciation

Period: ______________________________

Asset Description	Date of Acquisition	Original Price	Current Value	Depreciation Amount	Current Book Value

Fixed Assets Depreciation

Period: ____________________________

Asset Description	Date of Acquisition	Original Price	Current Value	Depreciatio n Amount	Current Book Value

Fixed Assets Depreciation

Period: ______________________________

Asset Description	Date of Acquisition	Original Price	Current Value	Depreciation Amount	Current Book Value

Fixed Assets Depreciation

Period: ______________________________

Asset Description	Date of Acquisition	Original Price	Current Value	Depreciatio n Amount	Current Book Value

Fixed Assets Depreciation

Period: ______________________________

Asset Description	Date of Acquisition	Original Price	Current Value	Depreciation Amount	Current Book Value

Fixed Assets Depreciation

Period: ______________________________

Asset Description	Date of Acquisition	Original Price	Current Value	Depreciation Amount	Current Book Value

Fixed Assets Depreciation

Period: ______________________________

Asset Description	Date of Acquisition	Original Price	Current Value	Depreciation Amount	Current Book Value

Fixed Assets Depreciation

Period: ______________________________

Asset Description	Date of Acquisition	Original Price	Current Value	Depreciatio n Amount	Current Book Value

Fixed Assets Depreciation

Period: ______________________________

Asset Description	Date of Acquisition	Original Price	Current Value	Depreciation Amount	Current Book Value

Fixed Assets Depreciation

Period: ______________________________

Asset Description	Date of Acquisition	Original Price	Current Value	Depreciatio n Amount	Current Book Value

Fixed Assets Depreciation

Period: ______________________________

Asset Description	Date of Acquisition	Original Price	Current Value	Depreciation Amount	Current Book Value

Fixed Assets Depreciation

Period: ______________________________

Asset Description	Date of Acquisition	Original Price	Current Value	Depreciatio n Amount	Current Book Value

Fixed Assets Depreciation

Period: ____________________________

Asset Description	Date of Acquisition	Original Price	Current Value	Depreciatio n Amount	Current Book Value

Fixed Assets Depreciation

Period: ______________________________

Asset Description	Date of Acquisition	Original Price	Current Value	Depreciatio n Amount	Current Book Value

Fixed Assets Depreciation

Period: ______________________________

Asset Description	Date of Acquisition	Original Price	Current Value	Depreciatio n Amount	Current Book Value

Fixed Assets Depreciation

Period: ______________________________

Asset Description	Date of Acquisition	Original Price	Current Value	Depreciation Amount	Current Book Value

Fixed Assets Depreciation

Period: ______________________________

Asset Description	Date of Acquisition	Original Price	Current Value	Depreciation Amount	Current Book Value

Fixed Assets Depreciation

Period: ______________________________

Asset Description	Date of Acquisition	Original Price	Current Value	Depreciation Amount	Current Book Value

Fixed Assets Depreciation

Period: ______________________________

Asset Description	Date of Acquisition	Original Price	Current Value	Depreciation Amount	Current Book Value

Fixed Assets Depreciation

Period: ______________________________

Asset Description	Date of Acquisition	Original Price	Current Value	Depreciation Amount	Current Book Value

Fixed Assets Depreciation

Period: ______________________________

Asset Description	Date of Acquisition	Original Price	Current Value	Depreciatio n Amount	Current Book Value

Fixed Assets Depreciation

Period: ______________________________

Asset Description	Date of Acquisition	Original Price	Current Value	Depreciatio n Amount	Current Book Value

Fixed Assets Depreciation

Period: ______________________________

Asset Description	Date of Acquisition	Original Price	Current Value	Depreciatio n Amount	Current Book Value

Fixed Assets Depreciation

Period: ______________________________

Asset Description	Date of Acquisition	Original Price	Current Value	Depreciation Amount	Current Book Value

Fixed Assets Depreciation

Period: ______________________________

Asset Description	Date of Acquisition	Original Price	Current Value	Depreciation Amount	Current Book Value

Fixed Assets Depreciation

Period: ______________________________

Asset Description	Date of Acquisition	Original Price	Current Value	Depreciation Amount	Current Book Value

Fixed Assets Depreciation

Period: ______________________________

Asset Description	Date of Acquisition	Original Price	Current Value	Depreciation Amount	Current Book Value

Fixed Assets Depreciation

Period: ______________________________

Asset Description	Date of Acquisition	Original Price	Current Value	Depreciatio n Amount	Current Book Value

Fixed Assets Depreciation

Period: ______________________________

Asset Description	Date of Acquisition	Original Price	Current Value	Depreciatio n Amount	Current Book Value

Fixed Assets Depreciation

Period: ______________________________

Asset Description	Date of Acquisition	Original Price	Current Value	Depreciation Amount	Current Book Value

Fixed Assets Depreciation

Period: ___________________________

Asset Description	Date of Acquisition	Original Price	Current Value	Depreciation Amount	Current Book Value

Fixed Assets Depreciation

Period: ____________________________

Asset Description	Date of Acquisition	Original Price	Current Value	Depreciation Amount	Current Book Value

Fixed Assets Depreciation

Period: ______________________________

Asset Description	Date of Acquisition	Original Price	Current Value	Depreciation Amount	Current Book Value

Fixed Assets Depreciation

Period: ______________________________

Asset Description	Date of Acquisition	Original Price	Current Value	Depreciation Amount	Current Book Value

Fixed Assets Depreciation

Period: ______________________________

Asset Description	Date of Acquisition	Original Price	Current Value	Depreciation Amount	Current Book Value

Fixed Assets Depreciation

Period: ______________________________

Asset Description	Date of Acquisition	Original Price	Current Value	Depreciatio n Amount	Current Book Value

Fixed Assets Depreciation

Period: ____________________________

Asset Description	Date of Acquisition	Original Price	Current Value	Depreciatio n Amount	Current Book Value

Fixed Assets Depreciation

Period: ______________________________

Asset Description	Date of Acquisition	Original Price	Current Value	Depreciatio n Amount	Current Book Value

Fixed Assets Depreciation

Period: ______________________________

Asset Description	Date of Acquisition	Original Price	Current Value	Depreciation Amount	Current Book Value

Fixed Assets Depreciation

Period: ______________________________

Asset Description	Date of Acquisition	Original Price	Current Value	Depreciation Amount	Current Book Value

Fixed Assets Depreciation

Period: ___________________________

Asset Description	Date of Acquisition	Original Price	Current Value	Depreciatio n Amount	Current Book Value

Fixed Assets Depreciation

Period: ______________________________

Asset Description	Date of Acquisition	Original Price	Current Value	Depreciation Amount	Current Book Value

Fixed Assets Depreciation

Period: ____________________________

Asset Description	Date of Acquisition	Original Price	Current Value	Depreciatio n Amount	Current Book Value

Fixed Assets Depreciation

Period: ____________________________

Asset Description	Date of Acquisition	Original Price	Current Value	Depreciation Amount	Current Book Value

Fixed Assets Depreciation

Period: ______________________________

Asset Description	Date of Acquisition	Original Price	Current Value	Depreciation Amount	Current Book Value

Fixed Assets Depreciation

Period: ____________________________

Asset Description	Date of Acquisition	Original Price	Current Value	Depreciatio n Amount	Current Book Value

Fixed Assets Depreciation

Period: ______________________________

Asset Description	Date of Acquisition	Original Price	Current Value	Depreciation Amount	Current Book Value

Fixed Assets Depreciation

Period: ____________________________

Asset Description	Date of Acquisition	Original Price	Current Value	Depreciation Amount	Current Book Value

Fixed Assets Depreciation

Period: ____________________________

Asset Description	Date of Acquisition	Original Price	Current Value	Depreciatio n Amount	Current Book Value

Fixed Assets Depreciation

Period: ______________________________

Asset Description	Date of Acquisition	Original Price	Current Value	Depreciation Amount	Current Book Value

Fixed Assets Depreciation

Period: ______________________________

Asset Description	Date of Acquisition	Original Price	Current Value	Depreciation Amount	Current Book Value

Fixed Assets Depreciation

Period: ______________________________

Asset Description	Date of Acquisition	Original Price	Current Value	Depreciatio n Amount	Current Book Value

Fixed Assets Depreciation

Period: ______________________________

Asset Description	Date of Acquisition	Original Price	Current Value	Depreciation Amount	Current Book Value

Fixed Assets Depreciation

Period: ______________________________

Asset Description	Date of Acquisition	Original Price	Current Value	Depreciatio n Amount	Current Book Value

Fixed Assets Depreciation

Period: ______________________________

Asset Description	Date of Acquisition	Original Price	Current Value	Depreciation Amount	Current Book Value

Fixed Assets Depreciation

Period: ______________________________

Asset Description	Date of Acquisition	Original Price	Current Value	Depreciation Amount	Current Book Value

Fixed Assets Depreciation

Period: ______________________________

Asset Description	Date of Acquisition	Original Price	Current Value	Depreciatio n Amount	Current Book Value

Fixed Assets Depreciation

Period: ______________________________

Asset Description	Date of Acquisition	Original Price	Current Value	Depreciation Amount	Current Book Value

Fixed Assets Depreciation

Period: ______________________________

Asset Description	Date of Acquisition	Original Price	Current Value	Depreciation Amount	Current Book Value

Fixed Assets Depreciation

Period: ______________________________

Asset Description	Date of Acquisition	Original Price	Current Value	Depreciatio n Amount	Current Book Value

Fixed Assets Depreciation

Period: ______________________________

Asset Description	Date of Acquisition	Original Price	Current Value	Depreciation Amount	Current Book Value

Fixed Assets Depreciation

Period: ______________________________

Asset Description	Date of Acquisition	Original Price	Current Value	Depreciation Amount	Current Book Value

Fixed Assets Depreciation

Period: ____________________________

Asset Description	Date of Acquisition	Original Price	Current Value	Depreciation Amount	Current Book Value

Fixed Assets Depreciation

Period: ______________________________

Asset Description	Date of Acquisition	Original Price	Current Value	Depreciation Amount	Current Book Value

Fixed Assets Depreciation

Period: ______________________________

Asset Description	Date of Acquisition	Original Price	Current Value	Depreciatio n Amount	Current Book Value

Fixed Assets Depreciation

Period: ______________________________

Asset Description	Date of Acquisition	Original Price	Current Value	Depreciation Amount	Current Book Value

Fixed Assets Depreciation

Period: ______________________________

Asset Description	Date of Acquisition	Original Price	Current Value	Depreciatio n Amount	Current Book Value

Fixed Assets Depreciation

Period: ______________________________

Asset Description	Date of Acquisition	Original Price	Current Value	Depreciatio n Amount	Current Book Value

Fixed Assets Depreciation

Period: ____________________________

Asset Description	Date of Acquisition	Original Price	Current Value	Depreciatio n Amount	Current Book Value

Fixed Assets Depreciation

Period: ______________________________

Asset Description	Date of Acquisition	Original Price	Current Value	Depreciation Amount	Current Book Value

Fixed Assets Depreciation

Period: ______________________________

Asset Description	Date of Acquisition	Original Price	Current Value	Depreciation Amount	Current Book Value

Fixed Assets Depreciation

Period: ______________________________

Asset Description	Date of Acquisition	Original Price	Current Value	Depreciation Amount	Current Book Value

Fixed Assets Depreciation

Period: ______________________________

Asset Description	Date of Acquisition	Original Price	Current Value	Depreciatio n Amount	Current Book Value

Fixed Assets Depreciation

Period: ____________________________

Asset Description	Date of Acquisition	Original Price	Current Value	Depreciation Amount	Current Book Value

Fixed Assets Depreciation

Period: ______________________________

Asset Description	Date of Acquisition	Original Price	Current Value	Depreciation Amount	Current Book Value

Fixed Assets Depreciation

Period: ___________________________

Asset Description	Date of Acquisition	Original Price	Current Value	Depreciation Amount	Current Book Value

Fixed Assets Depreciation

Period: ______________________________

Asset Description	Date of Acquisition	Original Price	Current Value	Depreciation Amount	Current Book Value

Fixed Assets Depreciation

Period: ______________________________

Asset Description	Date of Acquisition	Original Price	Current Value	Depreciatio n Amount	Current Book Value

Fixed Assets Depreciation

Period: ______________________________

Asset Description	Date of Acquisition	Original Price	Current Value	Depreciation Amount	Current Book Value

Fixed Assets Depreciation

Period: ______________________________

Asset Description	Date of Acquisition	Original Price	Current Value	Depreciatio n Amount	Current Book Value

Fixed Assets Depreciation

Period: ____________________________

Asset Description	Date of Acquisition	Original Price	Current Value	Depreciatio n Amount	Current Book Value

Fixed Assets Depreciation

Period: ______________________________

Asset Description	Date of Acquisition	Original Price	Current Value	Depreciation Amount	Current Book Value

Fixed Assets Depreciation

Period: ______________________________

Asset Description	Date of Acquisition	Original Price	Current Value	Depreciation Amount	Current Book Value

Fixed Assets Depreciation

Period: ______________________________

Asset Description	Date of Acquisition	Original Price	Current Value	Depreciation Amount	Current Book Value

Fixed Assets Depreciation

Period: ______________________________

Asset Description	Date of Acquisition	Original Price	Current Value	Depreciation Amount	Current Book Value

Fixed Assets Depreciation

Period: ______________________________

Asset Description	Date of Acquisition	Original Price	Current Value	Depreciation Amount	Current Book Value

Fixed Assets Depreciation

Period: ______________________________

Asset Description	Date of Acquisition	Original Price	Current Value	Depreciation Amount	Current Book Value

Fixed Assets Depreciation

Period: ______________________________

Asset Description	Date of Acquisition	Original Price	Current Value	Depreciation Amount	Current Book Value

Fixed Assets Depreciation

Period: ______________________________

Asset Description	Date of Acquisition	Original Price	Current Value	Depreciation Amount	Current Book Value

Fixed Assets Depreciation

Period: ______________________________

Asset Description	Date of Acquisition	Original Price	Current Value	Depreciation Amount	Current Book Value

Fixed Assets Depreciation

Period: ______________________________

Asset Description	Date of Acquisition	Original Price	Current Value	Depreciatio n Amount	Current Book Value

Fixed Assets Depreciation

Period: ______________________________

Asset Description	Date of Acquisition	Original Price	Current Value	Depreciatio n Amount	Current Book Value

Fixed Assets Depreciation

Period: ______________________________

Asset Description	Date of Acquisition	Original Price	Current Value	Depreciation Amount	Current Book Value

Fixed Assets Depreciation

Period: ______________________________

Asset Description	Date of Acquisition	Original Price	Current Value	Depreciation Amount	Current Book Value

Fixed Assets Depreciation

Period: ______________________________

Asset Description	Date of Acquisition	Original Price	Current Value	Depreciation Amount	Current Book Value

Fixed Assets Depreciation

Period: ______________________________

Asset Description	Date of Acquisition	Original Price	Current Value	Depreciatio n Amount	Current Book Value

Fixed Assets Depreciation

Period: ______________________________

Asset Description	Date of Acquisition	Original Price	Current Value	Depreciation Amount	Current Book Value

Fixed Assets Depreciation

Period: ______________________________

Asset Description	Date of Acquisition	Original Price	Current Value	Depreciation Amount	Current Book Value

Fixed Assets Depreciation

Period: ______________________________

Asset Description	Date of Acquisition	Original Price	Current Value	Depreciation Amount	Current Book Value

Fixed Assets Depreciation

Period: ______________________________

Asset Description	Date of Acquisition	Original Price	Current Value	Depreciation Amount	Current Book Value

Fixed Assets Depreciation

Period: ______________________________

Asset Description	Date of Acquisition	Original Price	Current Value	Depreciation Amount	Current Book Value

Fixed Assets Depreciation

Period: ______________________________

Asset Description	Date of Acquisition	Original Price	Current Value	Depreciation Amount	Current Book Value

Fixed Assets Depreciation

Period: ______________________________

Asset Description	Date of Acquisition	Original Price	Current Value	Depreciation Amount	Current Book Value

Fixed Assets Depreciation

Period: ______________________________

Asset Description	Date of Acquisition	Original Price	Current Value	Depreciation Amount	Current Book Value

Fixed Assets Depreciation

Period: ______________________________

Asset Description	Date of Acquisition	Original Price	Current Value	Depreciation Amount	Current Book Value

www.ingramcontent.com/pod-product-compliance
Lightning Source LLC
Chambersburg PA
CBHW080259180526
45167CB00006B/2585